All Scripture references taken from the KJV of the Holy Bible, unless otherwise indicated.

Idols Are Demons, Idols are Devils, Idols Are Little-g *gods*: *Why Is All This Stuff Happening To Me?*

by Dr. Marlene Miles

Freshwater Press 2024

freshwaterpress9@gmail.com

ISBN: 978-1-963164-76-3

Paperback Version

Copyright 2024, Dr. Marlene Miles

All rights reserved. No part of this book may be reproduced, distributed, or transmitted by any means or in any means including photocopying, recording or other electronic or mechanical methods without prior written permission of the publisher except in the case of brief publications or critical reviews.

Table of Contents

Invocation	4
One Fine Day	5
Make Sure You Are Saved	12
Why Am I Going *Through*?	13
The Journey Began	23
God Is Jealous	27
Idols are Demons, Idols are Devils, Idols are little-g *gods*	31
Harlotry	41
Foundational *Stuff*	49
The *gods* Must Be Crazy	53
Tests	62
Young Men Who Went to *School*	66
Help!	71
Just As We Are	76
Dear Reader	105
Other books by this author	106
Other Series	114
Prayer books by this author	117

Idols Are Demons, Idols are Devils, Idols Are Little-g *gods*

Why Is All This Stuff Happening to Me?

Freshwater Press, USA

Invocation

We pray the Lord will bless you as you read this book and that He will enlighten your understanding and bring you out of any problems you may have, into His marvelous light and that the *stuff* that keeps happening to you, will stop happening to you.

One Fine Day

One fine day you decided to get saved. The Lord pulled on your heartstrings, and it was time. You got saved. Hallelujah, Praise the Lord, AMEN.

You belong to God now, so that should solve everything, right?

Well, it *can* solve everything.

Joseph belonged to God and served God. Joseph is treated very badly by his own brothers, so just because you're saved doesn't mean that people will treat you well or even right--, even other professed-saved people. Joseph belonged to God. If he belonged to God, why is his family treating him this way? Doesn't the whole family belong to God and believe in God?

Joseph is sold into slavery. Joseph is sold into slavery by his own brothers who are also supposed to be serving God.

What?

The brothers' jealousy, surely. But that Joseph was sold into slavery by his brothers proves that relatives can sell you into slavery. Because your guard is down with relatives, this may afford the most evil of your kinfolk to have access to you to do evil against you. The same applies to friends, that you may find out later on are actually fake friends.

A friend loveth at all times, and a brother is born for adversity. (Proverbs 17:17)

I don't know about you, but Joseph's ordeal helps me understand why I've heard people wish they were the only children of their parents.

After being sold into slavery and now living in Egypt, Joseph was accosted by Potiphar's wife and rejected her, so he ends up in prison. Egypt typifies the world and sin; this also proves that relatives, even brothers can sell you out into sin. Don't believe everything anyone tells you; try everything by the Word of God. People have been tricked, led, or caused to fall into prison by those they love and or trust as a brother.

But Joseph belongs to God. Joseph did right to not sin with a married woman, so how did the kind of *stuff* that happened to Joseph, happen to Joseph?

You belong to God, don't you? Do strange or odd things happen to you? You may not be associated with anyone who is leading you into sin or evil. You may be serving God to the utmost—but do things happen to you that you know shouldn't be happening to a child of God?

Daniel belonged to God, but Daniel ends up a prisoner of war – in captivity. Daniel was in collective captivity with Judah because of their unrepented rebellion and sin against God. Sometimes that is the reason that even innocent or good people go *through--*, collective captivity. In today's terms we see it as hanging out with the wrong crowd, or being in the wrong place when a crime goes down and innocent joyriders may end up in jail also.

As with Joseph, who receives harsh punishment for not doing wrong, Daniel gets thrown into a lion's den and a fiery furnace because Daniel won't bow to the idol when the music is played. But Daniel belongs to God; why would Daniel get in trouble for doing right by God?

Don't you also belong to God? Then crazy things ought not to be happening to you.

Job belonged to God and was upright before Him, but Job really went *through*.

There are so many recounts in the Bible of God's people going through things, mostly for doing wrong. However, by the Divine plan of God folks can do right and still end up in bad situations. Joseph, Daniel, Job, and Jesus.

Joseph, Daniel, and Job got hardships and tests beyond. When you read their stories, you may think this is too much. We have tests, trials and tribulations ourselves, hopefully they are not as extreme as those mentioned. We are to share in the suffering of Christ. The Bible says we are to take up our cross daily, but none of us expect to go through what Jesus went through and be crucified. Take up your cross means that if you are in Christ, then lay down your flesh life and walk by the Spirit, not fulfilling the lusts of this world. Chasing after flesh desires is what gets everyone into spiritual trouble.

Saved, walking upright before God and being moral and ethical means we should be experiencing the best treatment and best outcomes in our life. *Right*?

You're saved but might be wondering why you're going through so much. It's not just because you're saved, but it is because you've chosen a different path than most, a different path than the world. It may look as though others are doing fine and maybe they are, maybe they aren't. It may just appear that way from the outside looking in.

Others are probably in the world serving their *god or gods from the world*. That doesn't mean that they won't be going through, but those who are fully in the world's system are on their way to hell anyway, so the devil doesn't mess with them as much as he loves to bother God's people.

Why? To traumatize God's people, to provoke them to desperation, misery, sin, failure—anything to compromise them so they will sin, so he can then attack them further to either steal, kill, or destroy them.

Notice though that those who are in the world are working the world's system. Christians are in the world working God's system. Do you think the world will like that? Do you think the devil will like that. Of course, not. The fact that you are not behaving as the rest of the world probably riles the devil and he may come to antagonize you for antagonizing him.

Yet we remain in Christ, we serve God, walking after the Spirit.

Make Sure You Are Saved

Father, I believe that Jesus is the Son of God and that He came to Earth and died to take my sins to the Cross. I believe that on the third day You resurrected Jesus from the grave and that He lives!

I believe in my heart, and I confess with my mouth unto repentance by faith and by the Grace of God. I invite Jesus into my heart and into my life to be the Lord of my Life and I believe today that I am saved, in the Name of Jesus.

Amen.

Why Am I Going *Through*?

On that fine day when you got saved, or accepted the Lord, you became accountable to Jehovah God, responsible to know the Word of God, responsible to hear the voice of God, and do what the Word and what God says.

You may not hear the voice of God, but those inclinations and nudges that God gives you by His Spirit is God's way of guiding and instructing you. This could be why you're going *through*, if you're not following those inklings and nudges. How many people say, *Something told me to go this way and not that way*? Yes, that some*thing* is a **person**; He is the Holy Spirit. This is how God guides and protects us. Others, and you also may learn to hear the voice of God who speaks to us all day, in many ways.

If you are saved and just being saved and doing nothing else, and nothing else differently than how you used to do things before you got saved, this could be why you're going *through*.

I used to think that being saved meant that I've checked off that box, now I can go back to whatever I was doing. I used to think I could even keep on doing what my friends, who are not saved are doing, because they were still my friends, weren't they?

Even though they weren't saved, they were still my friends, right? Just because I got saved, did that mean that I was supposed to change *friends*? I had received salvation, which to me meant I now had God-insurance and that was for later, but right now I was still hanging out with my pals and running buddies.

Thinking life is an adventure to live as you please--, well, that's what the world tells us, especially from Madison Avenue. Even in some of churchdom we are taught that once you accept Jesus as the Lord of your life, everything is now fine.

Truth is, you weren't your own before you got saved. Once you accept Jesus you are now bought with a price and that price is Jesus Christ. If you were bought with a price that means you were sold.

Who sold you?

The person (entity) that owned you.

Who owned you?

The world. The devil. The dark kingdom. Before you accept Christ, by default, you already belong to the devil; it is default in the Earth. Your parents may have christened you as a baby, but until you reach the age of accountability and accept Jesus Christ for yourself, you are not saved. You may have been sprinkled with water--, holy or otherwise it doesn't matter. You could have been sprinkled with tap water, bottled water, fizzy water, it doesn't matter you are not saved by that sprinkling of a little water by a priest or a pastor. You are not saved as a baby because you were not able to make a conscious decision for Christ at that time.

As an infant, maybe you had a Baby Dedication, but that is not salvation or baptism into Christ. That is your parents and the grown people in your life promising to raise you up in the fear and admonition of the Lord. No one really checks later on, to see if they are doing that, if they simply drop out of sight, or out of church. Some only come to church for Baby Dedication and may not even be saved themselves. So, how are they to bring a baby up in the fear and admonition of the Lord, when they don't fear the Lord, or know Him themselves?

Praise God, at some of these baby dedications I've seen the parents and other relatives accept Christ right on the spot. Well, Praise God and Amen.

Serving idols, false *gods*, and the kingdom of darkness is built into being born on Earth until you accept Christ. A person cannot inherit salvation from their saved grandmother, but they can inherit being a witch from either parent, or worse, both parents. They can be initiated into witchcraft or occultism, without even knowing it, by anyone, a relative or a stranger. There is so much sin and darkness in this world, it is only by the Mercy of God that we are not all consumed, daily. Recall from Revelations 18 that Babylon trades in slaves and the souls of men. That means that souls are bought and sold every day; it is commonplace to Babylon, the dark kingdom.

Ye are bought with a price because every time you sin you sell your own soul. Ye are bought with a price because others can sell you into sin and into the dark kingdom. Ye are bought with a price when you want to come back from having been nominated as a candidate for sacrifice and you did nothing about it until the very last moment. Thank God, you realized it and began to call on the Lord. After hearing your prayers, the Lord now has to buy you back with the Blood of Jesus.

Ye are bought with a price because we are all born into sin and shaped in iniquity; it is already in our bloodline and depending on our foundation, we could already be in hock spiritually before we even get here. So, there is no way that you are saved when you are born, you are not saved as an infant, you are not saved until you accept Christ and become saved.

You are not your own even now—none of us are; you are bought with a price. Your soul has been purchased back from hell, death, grave, or from some evil altar that a witch or some evil ancestors put you on—, whomever has it. An evil ancestor could have put you on an evil altar and if that altar is still being attended to it will continue to fire against you. The demons sent to enforce the evil covenant that your ancestor may have made in ignorance or arrogance are sent to make sure that you keep going through *stuff;* they are sent to punish you. You may be going through unbelievable, ridiculous, even heinous or grievous *stuff* because of evil altars, current altars, or ancient altars.

Ancient altars projecting against your family means that everyone in your bloodline up to now may have gone through the same things. What are the common patterns of disease, affliction or suffering in your family? Most likely those cyclical and generational events are because of an evil altar emanating against your bloodline.

The *stuff* I used to go through was so unbelievable that people thought I was making up some of the things that would happen to me. In my naivete I thought that things would just settle down on their own and after I finished school, or got married, or did whatever goal I had set for myself that things would just level out.

I was hoping by whatever law states that if something has already gone wrong, it can't go wrong again. Kind of akin to lightning not striking twice in the same place. Folks, neither of those things are true, unless God is in it and tells you that the enemies you see today, you shall see them no more, things won't just settle down on their own. Lightning can strike again in the same place and the same wrong things can happen and rehappen to a person, a family, a bloodline if evil covenants are in place and evil is programmed seasonally or cyclically in an altar that has mounted itself against your family.

Hope springs eternal, but hoping won't make evil patterns stop. It takes prayer, sometimes fasting, and also deliverance to make *stuff* stop happening to you. I'm especially thinking about things that you know you have done nothing, personally to cause.

Demons do not get tired. They are relentless because they are driven by fear to do what the devil tells them to do. They also have no flesh bodies and do not get tired as humans do. They don't stop. Over time, they get stronger, so they must be stopped as soon as you are aware that they are in your life, in your soul, and affecting your successes and outcomes.

You get saved; now, Jesus comes into your life. Hallelujah!

Many think that God lives *at church* like a grandmother or grandfather who lives in a house down the way from you, and you go see them when you want – like once a month or so.

Nope, When you got saved, you asked the LORD into your heart and into your life.

Can you imagine asking a friend over to your house and you totally ignore them the whole time they are there?

So, you've asked God into your heart—and Jesus showed up. Amen. You are not ignoring God, are you? You are not ignoring His nudges or inclinations, are you? That could explain why you are going through all kinds of *stuff*.

The Journey Began

When you got saved you began a spiritual journey that actually began whether you began it or not. It is a hard concept to think that a spiritual journey that started **because of you** could have started *without* you.

It could have started without you and left you right where you were—at that altar, in that living room, soaking from that baptismal pool, or wherever you got saved. You got that far, but did you take the next step of the journey? The journey began, but did you begin the journey?

Or are you still in the world, with your friends still playing around and not being serious about God, or life, but the journey has started. Are you not on this journey?

That could be why you're going through. This is why *stuff* keeps happening to you.

When you got saved, you begin in spiritual school I'll call it – the school bell rang – did you hear it? The bell rang and it was time to convene inside. You were called into the classroom; did you go into the *school*?

This could be why you are now going *through*.

We are to study to show ourselves approved. Have you been studying and showing yourself approved? God does not want us ignorant.

> Because of a lack of knowledge, God's people perish. (Hosea 4:6)

School began because you got saved; school began **for you** because you got saved. You are anointed to be saved, you are anointed when you get saved, and now you are also anointed now to ***become***.

Become what?

Whatever God says you are to become. And that takes training, education, experiences, going *through* sometimes. tests and trials sometimes, in God, that is, **_with_** God. That is not you alone, twisting in the wind. It takes relationship. Because God is with you, God's at your house and everywhere you go; He is Omnipresent. Are you talking to Him? God is listening to you and listening for you.

Are you listening to Him? Are you inclining to His Word? He talks through His Word. Aside from the nudges, inklings, urges, and inclinations, God talks through dreams and visions. God talks through people, teachers, prophets, pastors, all of the five-fold ministry. God is speaking to you.

He walks with you, and He talks with you because He not only loves you, He is in love with you. God is in love with you; you are accepted in the Beloved.

And here you thought you had no one who loves you, when God is loving you like that, that deeply.

God Is Jealous

Case in point; God is *in love* with you and He is Jealous. When people love you, they love you. It's kind of a live and let live relationship; they want the best for you, but not in a possessive way. But when a person is **IN LOVE** with you, that's when you may see jealousy.

There are many types of jealousy, and the world has labeled types of jealousy. Romantic jealousy, Power jealousy, Sexual jealousy, Pathological or irrational, or morbid jealousy, family jealousy and rational jealousy.

God cannot be put into any of those categories. Godly jealousy comes from God loving us with a perfect love and expecting us to love him the same way, as much as it is humanly possible.

God is jealous *over* you. Look at what you cost God. Does God put value on you and then pay what He deems that value to be, or did He pay for you and then realize the value. God and every wise man begin with the end in mind. So, when God said, Let us go down and make man in our own image and likeness He already knew what value would be on man.

When man sinned, God knew what He was willing to pay to buy man back from death, destruction and hell. God already knew the value of His Masterpiece, what he had fearfully and wonderfully made and created a little lower than Elohim.

> For I am jealous over you with godly jealousy: for I have espoused you to one husband, that I may present you as a chaste virgin to Christ.
> (2 Corinthians 11:2-3)

Saints of God when you put value on a thing, when you have value on a thing, you guard it, protect it, cherish it, keep it, and you are JEALOUS over it. God is Jealous *over* us.

So why are you going *through*?

Because **GOD is Jealous**. He says He is a Jealous God. So, if you are out in the world playing with your friends, but you've invited God into your heart and into your life but you are distracted by the cares of this world, how do you think God will feel?

If you went on a date with a person and they spent the whole date talking to the hostess at the restaurant, making jokes with the waiter, leaning over to the table beside you to chat with the couple at the table next to yours, but didn't include you in any of the interactions and didn't pay any attention to you, would you want to see that person again?

If your friend invited you over to their house but ignored you and kept doing what they were doing before you got there, playing on their game console, looking at their cellphone, watching TV, watching sports?

You got saved. You invited God into your life. Do you have faith enough and love enough for God to spend time with Him and acknowledge His presence, at least? Don't let ignoring God be the reason that you are going *through*.

God is Jealous.

Idols are Demons, Idols are Devils, Idols are little-g *gods*

Another reason you may be going through is that all *gods* are jealous – even the little g *gods*. They want your time, your attention and your worship. This doesn't mean that if you are a jealous person, you are a god; please don't think like that.

But because Jehovah God is Jealous. One fine day you got saved and invited God into your heart and your life to be the Lord of your life – might as well say, to be the LOVE of your life because none of us have LOVE for anything or anyone unless we get it from God; for God is Love.

The first commandment that God gave man was that he should have no other *gods*, no other idols.

And God spoke all these words:

"I am the LORD your God, who brought you out of Egypt, out of the land of slavery.

"You shall have no other gods before me." (Exodus 20:2)

The people of God got in more trouble in the Bible for chasing after, seeking after, serving and worshipping idols than for anything else.

Idols are demons. Idols are devils, idols are little g *gods*.

Why are you going through?

It's because of your idols.

What idols? Uh huh; don't play innocent. Your music celebrities. Your sports stars. You name brand clothing. Your name brand cars, handbags, anything. Your good luck charms. Your traditional practices, rituals, food. Your holidays, holiday gifts, parades, costumes, activities, and et cetera.

It's your idols--, the idols of your father's house. It is why things keep *happening* to you and you keep going through *stuff.*

My father's house?

Yes, idols are inherited. Traditions are cultivated. Family habits are taught, encouraged, nurtured and practiced. What child would ever want to put on a Halloween costume unless their parent or someone had not presented it to them when they were a toddler and convinced them that it was okay, or fun?

Idols are little g *gods*

The idols you used to serve before that one fine day when you got saved, they **are mad at you** for defecting, for leaving them, for rejecting them and not continuing to worship them. Idols, are in your life and your soul to lead you to take on their nature. They are full of sin and desire to lead you into living a life of sin. That's the first step, after that they can have more access to everything they want to steal from you, keep from you, as they destroy your life and you with it.

Idols in the soul of a person is why people behave or misbehave the way they do.

Not only that, they know that Jehovah is mightier, bigger and stronger than they are or could ever hope to be. They are first of all, jealous *of* God because He is God. You know a person is jealous of you when they are trying to take or destroy what is yours, when they are trying to impersonate Him.

They mutinied more than once, but that time they did it in Heaven is when they got kicked out. They are trying to take you from God, although God says that no one can take you out of His hand. Furthermore, shouldn't it be obvious if God kicked them out of Heaven that we should not be hosting them? If God kicked them out, then we should do the same.

Don't you feel a certain way when your friends remain friends with your former friends? Yeah, we got that from God. God says that your enemy is His enemy, therefore because we are saved and in covenant with God, shouldn't His enemies also be our enemies? Idols are fallen angels, they are demons, idols are devils, idols are little-g *gods* who want to **be** God.

Sadly, you can take yourself out of God's hand unless you are among the very elite and cannot be deceived.

Demons are jealous of you because mankind has authority and dominion in the Earth, and because mankind can be redeemed, demons can't—they are doomed. In the natural, if someone is jealous of you, do you not realize how dangerous they are? God is in love with you and demons are jealous of you. If you are in your right mind, which would you choose to be with? To serve? To worship? To Host? Demons, devils, and idols, or the Holy Spirit of God?

However, even though man was kicked out of Paradise, kicked out of the Garden of Eden—demons are fallen angels who were kicked out of Heaven. As nice as the Garden of Eden was--, Eden versus Heaven? Take a moment and think about this.

They made the worst mistake of their existence when they rebelled against their Creator and fell from the Third Heaven to Earth, where they had rule and dominion, until God created man and put man here on Earth in that position. **Now, man has authority over demons, to subdue them, and really to kick demons out of the Earth.** Demons are desperate and fighting for their evil lives. If you are not subduing them, they will subdue you. If you are not taking authority over them, they will run all over you. If you are not taking dominion over them, they will take dominion over you.

You cannot co-exist with demons; don't let them deceive you. They may have you thinking that they are making your happier, have more fun, and smarter. All the while they are imparting their sin nature to you to sink you deeper into sin and destruction.

You want to lord over something? Lord over demons. You want to be the boss of something? Be the boss of demons. You want to show somebody that you're the man? You are the man, and you have authority over demons. Take it. Use it.

So, these jealous devils--, folks think about this, you know jealous people, relatives, friends, coworkers, that is nothing compared to a jealous demon who most likely are the pathologically jealous types. People who take on their nature exhibit the worst kinds of jealousy. That leads to the worst outcomes. Cain was pathologically, morbidly jealous of Abel.

Any of the demon's goal is to keep you distracted, poor, sick, going through. To keep you from realizing a good relationship with God Almighty, and that you can be increased and strengthened and grown and walk worthy of your calling and take your position of dominion over *them*.

But they want to distract you so you never figure that out, so they can stay in your life, in your very soul, and in your bloodline. Because that is how most of them got there, through your ancestry and your bloodline.

Now, this is where you and your actions or lack of action determines what is happening to you in your life. If you are lightly esteeming God, if you've gotten saved, but just saved and not doing much else, then a Christian can still have demons. If you've invited God into your life but you aren't living your life as if God is in it, the jealous little g *gods* are not only furious with you, they are vengeful, and realize that you are either powerless or not as powerful as you can be, so they will come at you every kind of way and punish you, just because they can.

In addition to that, they are afraid of God, afraid of your relationship with God, and afraid that you will realize who you are in God and kick them out of your life and your soul. They are desperate. So, if you are only loosely *associated* with God, have a dry prayer life and little faith, the demons can run all over you. And, if they can, they will.

Dear Reader: That is why you are going through so much.

Harlotry

Again, Dear Reader: You accepted Jesus Christ as the Lord of your life, invited Him into your heart – over to your house. Are you ignoring Him? Are you two-timing, or three-timing God? Are you cheating on Him with idols--, other things that demand your time, attention, money, sacrifices, and your worship?

The *gods* of your father's house are the ones you inherited, along with your sin nature --- we all are born into it. Your sin nature comes from the demons in your soul. Their goal is to get you to take on their nature; their nature is sin. It is what comes natural to them. In addition to the ones we were born with, we've picked up idols (little g *gods*) by our own sins – either random sins or sins that we do because **it is in our blood** to do them. Until you get saved, it is in your blood to do what the idols from your father's house tell you to do. Whatever you saw your parents doing, even if you hate it and detest it, without Jesus Christ you are going to do it.

If a person never gets saved, they are going to do what their folks before them did because it is:

1. In their blood to do those things.

2. There are markers in their blood that draw sins to them.

Like father like son? Yeah, it's more like blood-like blood. When you've got the same blood coursing through your veins, **without** spiritual help from the Lord, you will do what has been programmed into your blood for centuries.

Like mother like daughter? Sometimes. This thing is not gender-specific, but it is like parent-like child. Some say it's the DNA, and it is, but it is the blood that tells the DNA how to express itself. It is in the blood.

That's why all your friends are the same. All your friendships turn out the same. That's why you keep attracting the same type of boyfriend or girlfriend – it's in **your** blood, if you haven't gotten saved, and fully converted. You can be saved and still be drawing people, situations and temptations by the markers in your blood, in your soul if you have not fully put on Christ.

If you **have** gotten saved, but you haven't fully *converted* to Christ – your blood is still speaking, calling, drawing stuff, things, situations, and people, and sin and punishments to you to repeat those cycles over and again.

If you have gotten saved and have not fully put on Christ, you are in a nebulous, dangerous, neither here nor there place. God says that He would rather you be hot or cold—not lukewarm. If you are saved and have put on Christ, you are hot. If you are not saved, you are cold--, at least cold toward God; you might be hot for sin and hell. Your *hotness* could be the exact temperature of hell, for all you know; that could be why you are attracting hellish things into your life.

Get saved. Today.

If you are saved and have not fully appropriated and put on the new man in Christ, you are lukewarm.

And what does being lukewarm mean to God?

Lukewarm is something to be spit out of God's mouth.

Saved, as in name only, or on paper, but your body is still in the world with your worldly friends doing the worldly things that leave you in a place where the idol *gods* will attack; that is spiritually lukewarm. If you have no real spiritual covering because you are not walking upright before the Lord, that is spiritually lukewarm. Let the Lord help you; He is the only one who can.

You may say you want Christ, but you are still on the fence. Do you know how hard it is to balance on a fence? So on the fence you are unbalanced which means you are not stable, we will say spiritually stable. But what is spiritual will manifest physically sooner or later.

There is a young woman who realizes that she is under spiritual attack by the things that happen in her physical life, and by her dreams. Just last week, in the natural, the brother of one of her so-called *friends*, along with some other thugs tried to carjack her car while she was in it.

She is Catholic to the max and cannot wrap her mind around getting saved and being a real Christian. She still wants rosary beads, little statues of saints and a bigger statue of Mary, who is the Queen of the Coast, and she has been told this, but she cannot hear this right now. She is in love with the Virgin Mary who went on to have four or five other kids after Jesus, so she was no longer a virgin. Furthermore, Mary was a mortal who is dead and did not get resurrected as Christ did. The Queen of the Coast garners worship by pretending to be the Virgin Mary and getting millions of Catholics to worship "her." The Queen of the Coast is a demon, purported to be the wife of Satan.

So, this young Catholic woman spends money on fresh cut flowers to put on her home "altar" in front of this statue of the "virgin Mary" every week.

When I go in the grocery store and see the lovely flowers, I wonder who the lucky women are whose men bring them flowers every week or at least regularly. Now I know, it is the Queen of the Coast who is getting flowers every week. A demon is getting flowers every week. This is disturbing to me.

What's worse is this woman does not want salvation in Christ Jesus, but the demons she is serving are not serving her, they are attacking her and destroying her life. Just last week she dreamed of being snake-bitten. Christ has been presented but her hardened heart, which basically wants to party "is not ready." Her blood is pre-programmed to party; it has come through her generations, and she has not and cannot give it a thought because she can't see it. All her family is that way and all her friends are that way, upholding the stronghold that keeps her in the yokes of sin.

Folks we all better call on the Lord while He may be found.

All of what is happening to the woman is FOUNDATION STUFF; it is foundational ISSUES, and those things are expressed in the blood.

Foundational *Stuff*

You're different than that woman who wants to keep sinning. You've invited Jesus into your heart and into your life. It seems the first thing Jesus would deal with is your foundation. Have you done that? Do you expect that you will ever do that? What does that even mean? Where do you start?

It should be pretty sobering to think that what is wrong in your life is because of **your** foundation. We all want to play the blame game sometimes--, this person did this to me, that person, my parents, and of course, the ancestors who aren't even here to defend themselves.

But we have to look at our own stuff, our own foundation. You may think: *Am I that jacked up?*

Maybe.

It's why we need salvation; we are born into sin, we are born with iniquity, we are born with idols from our father's house, our mother's house. We inherit those things, and they are in our blood to make us that way and keep repeating the same cycles until the Lord says otherwise, and by your agreement with the Lord, you say otherwise.

Dealing with foundations in the natural, folks there are sinkholes and there are faulty foundations, there are sinking sands.(Matthew 7:24)

These are all foundation issues that must be dealt with. We may think we want God to come in and deal with all the obvious stuff in our lives – obvious to us--, the stuff that we see, such as pain in the body, sicknesses, lack, poverty. It is the hidden stuff that causes what we see. It is foundational iniquity hidden in the foundation that are the source of problems we experience in the natural. That is why we deal with the **foundation**.

The one the builders rejected has become the Chief Cornerstone. If Jesus knows how to be the chief cornerstone and we need foundation work, we'd be foolish not to accept His ability to BE our foundation.

The stone which the builders refused is become the headstone of the corner. This is the LORD's doing; It is marvellous in our eyes.
(Psalms 118:22-23)

Jesus is also named Capstone.

Unless the Lord build the house they that labor, labor in vain.

Jesus is both the Capstone and Cornerstone of our lives (Psalm 118:22). The cornerstone brings stability and support when everything else feels shaky.

The capstone, holds all the broken pieces together and completes what is unfinished and imperfect. When we have a good foundation and a stable building, we can get off the fence that is so unstable.

We invite the LORD into our lives, but do we just want the idea of Him being around, yet continue to ignore Him when there is so much work to do?

God is here to work out stuff in your life, but we can't treat Him as if He's our maid or a handyman giving *Him* instructions or directions on what to do instead of listening to Him, this could be why stuff—crazy stuff keeps happening to you. It could be why you're going *through.*

The *gods* Must Be Crazy

The *gods* must be crazy – well their jealous, they are desperate. They think you belong to them, especially if you haven't renounced them, broken up with them. The little g *gods* that you were born serving are the idols of your father's house. Because of the anger, rage, uproar and riot of the idols in your soul—in your life – that is why you are going *through*.

How many of you have ever had a desperate, jealous boyfriend or girlfriend? Yeah, idol *gods* are like that. The idol *gods* are the one that drove that, hopefully ex of yours to behave that way. They fully sponsor works of the flesh in people. These idol *gods* contribute to the cray cray things that happen to you, such as your car being keyed, getting one or more flat tires, receiving 70 phone calls or text messages because you are not answering, evil social media posts, including revenge porn. Folks, keep your clothes on and stop sexting and sending pictures to folks who don't deserve to spy out your liberties. (Galatians 2:4)

The difference is the idol *gods* have a certain level of power that an *ex, in his own flesh,* doesn't have to make anything from inappropriate stuff, all the way to crazy things occurring in your life. This could be why things keep happening to you.

The only answer to this is to be all in with Christ and all in to Christ and be <u>fully converted.</u>

When we get saved, I've heard no one say all the things you will have to go through and need to do. We are simply led to the altar and we think everything will be instantly fixed. Coming up to the altar maybe the process by which Salvation is ministered to us, but as far as fixing all the stuff that we've messed up or accepted in our souls, this is only a start, and thank God for the start. Now we have the authority to *become* a son of God. When a new baby is born to the Smith family, it is a baby, then a child, then a teen and somewhere around 20 years later, that child has grown into a full son--, physically. It may take longer than 20 years, say a lifetime, but if we get saved as teens, 20 years is a generous amount of time to get spiritual schooling well underway toward becoming a true son of God.

When you are saved and born into the family of God, you are not a full grown son the next day, and especially if you do nothing and do not practice the disciplines to become fully grown, spiritually.

We just keep living until some time has gone by and we may be noticing that things have gone sideways or have gone nowhere at all. Things may even be stagnant, and we may be wondering why things are just not right. We may realize that we may need deliverance, if we haven't gone through the process of renouncing and denouncing all of the idols in our souls.

It would be fine to have complete deliverance when we accept salvation – and it is possible, depending on what is in you when you invite Christ in. We are not often taken through a full **renunciation** of whatever we used to do, what *gods* we used to serve before we invited and accepted Christ into our lives.

So we, erroneously, think that what we used to do is fine because no one ever literally told us, most of the time to STOP. We are told the obvious stuff such as drinking, smoking, chasing women, chasing men, but there are other sins. We may think it is okay, until we find out it is not okay.

We can find out what is not okay by teaching, by reading the Word, or by chaos erupting in our spiritual or physical life--, or both. We usually realize that we need **deliverance** when something hurts, or we lose something we dearly want or need—especially relationships and or money. We may find out what demons are still in us by our outward behavior and or circumstances, or if you are standing before a genuine seer or hearer and they are ministering to you to advise you on what is in your foundation or bloodline that you need to deal with.

Else, we all believe that all the ways of a man are clean in his own eyes and we think we are fine if the pastor told us to stop drinking and we did. In our eyes we are clean; people usually can't see their own mess and need for deliverance.

We may think what we used to do we can still do with our friends--, you know those same friends that we kept in spite of being saved, but we are not witnessing to them at all. We are using the as an excuse to foray out into the world and party hearty on Friday night. Then we sit like pious nuns and priests in church on Sunday mornings as if we are not culpable because our friends made us do it, and we didn't lead the charge to order a whole pitcher of margaritas.

We may think that whatever we did last night, at night on any night was okay because we are now saved and we are not in the church building right now, and we have accepted Christ, and we are going to visit God in the church where He lives, on Sunday anyway. One man was proud to say that he would never drink alcohol on church grounds---, okay, but he drinks everywhere else six days a week?

We are not realizing that God is where we live and everywhere we are, even that man who used to be a deacon at that church that he'd never drink at.

We expect that Jesus will fix what we do on these Friday nights, even more than we expect that He will save our friends who don't even want to be saved, and are trying to pull you back into the lifestyle that they are currently in and trying to perfect their sin life by continuing to sin most egregiously.

We expect that He is going to come into our hearts and shine a really bright light and al the roaches will scatter. Well, God is Light. Is He shining in you? He came over to your house/heart but you are not paying any attention to Him… God is Light but do you have Him sitting somewhere in the dark recesses of your mind as if He is an idol or a good luck charm, a mr. fix it when you need something fixed.

God said that you should have no idols before Him – it should go without being said that you don't treat God as if *He* is a mere idol.

How disrespectful. Lord, forgive us, in the Name of Jesus.

How do you treat idols?

- Some you pursue after hard when you want something from them.
- Then you can put them down at will because they are idols.
- But that is part of the problem, idols have tantrums like screaming babies when you put them down, only, unlike babies, they are evil enough and big enough and powerful enough to get revenge on you. That could be why you're going *through* right now—some of your one-night stands, very brief relationships, or situationships with *idols*.
- You pick them up at will because they are idols.

- Our God is not an idol, and He deserves a whole other level of respect; He deserves your time, attention, and worship.

God says that He will never leave or forsake you, but how long would you sit around at someone's house, someone who invited you over but you ignored them for hours and hours and days, even weeks, or months at a time?

This could be why you're going through, and why *stuff* keeps happening to you.

Tests

God knows what He has called you to *become*, and the clock started that one fine day you got saved and accepted Jesus. *School* convened that day, because God took you seriously, He took you at your word when you came down to that altar and made your confession of faith. God believed that you would put your hand to the plow and not turn back, you know, to go into the streets with your unsaved family members and *friends*.

Now, it's been five years, ten years or more and you are now getting tests commensurate with where you *should be* in Christ right now, based on when you got saved and what/who God called you to be when He formed you and when you accepted Christ into your heart and into your life.

School started that day and now the teaching is on the fifth grade or tenth grade level and you are still outside the kindergarten classroom and haven't even gone into the building yet.

Your current spiritual tests match where you *should be* in Christ right now. If you've been saved for some time, whether you've been studying the Word, praying, practicing the disciplines of the faith, or not, your current tests are at the level where you should be right now, in Him. Your expected level is also based on who you are called to be in the Kingdom.

Some have more schooling to do than others based on calling, and also based on where you started. You may have had to unlearn a lot of false and erroneous doctrine first. This is particular between you and God. With God, if you have tests and fail, then you keep getting those tests until you pass. The further you are behind where you should be spiritually the more those tests look like trials and tribulations.

You may be asking, Why is this happening to me? Why am I going through *this*? Like multiplication and division in the third grade, you can do it, but in kindergarten you cannot. Your tests match where you should be; they may seem very difficult if you haven't studied to show yourself approved, and especially if you haven't even stepped foot into the *school*.

Another person who may have gotten saved when you did may have entered school on schedule and may find that those little tests that come along in life are nothing. He knows what to do, how to pray, how to handle things. Conversely the one who has not studied is running to folks to get someone to help them, and even pray *for* them. I am in no way saying that you should not ask people to pray for you, but that should be to pray with you, or as an intercessor. We should not be asking people to pray instead of us praying ourselves.

Let's get caught up in our prayer lives, saints of God, and not be dry Christians.

Young Men Who Went to *School*

Daniel had to deal with a whole principality – who was not fighting Daniel but was holding up the answers to Daniel's prayers. Daniel was just a little Hebrew boy--- yeah in the natural, but to God Daniel was so much more.

Additionally, Daniel was prayerful, prayed up and fasted and had a right relationship with God, so when a principality came to delay his answers to prayers, Daniel had the moxie to handle it. But wait--, a whole principality was sent against Daniel. A *spiritual* kindergartner would not have known what to do in that circumstance. When Daniel met God, he went to **school**, folks, so by the time he was a teenager, in captivity, he still knew how to do warfare against a principality that was doing warfare against him.

Can you say the same? At 17, I could not say that I had a clue about any of that.

Joseph ended up being second in command after Pharaoh. Joseph's tests and trials were so severe because of who he would be to the plan of God. Further, it was also very telling in how Joseph handled himself with his brothers, as a slave, as an accused man, and as a prisoner that lets you know Joseph knew God and walked with God and God was with him.

How about you? What's your spiritual grade level? Can you imagine where you would be spiritually right now if you had, in earnest, started spiritual school when you got saved and had never once been discouraged from your path, or ever got derailed, tricked or backslid? Can you imagine where you would be spiritually right now?

- Oh Lord, redeem the time and restore the years, in the Name of Jesus.

We all need a strong healthy relationship with God so that when/if the unforeseen happens or if we are suddenly going *through*, we don't have to call on God, but He is already walking with you. You can just talk to Him and ask him. Lord, be with me through this, Lord, fight for me. You can just ask Him, and we can get through the trials of life --

Call on me while I can be found...

> Seek ye the LORD while he may be found, call ye upon him while he is near:
> (Isaiah 55:6)

A wise man is in hot pursuit of GOD as often as he can, not just when he has a problem or wants God to do something for him. God is not just for the fivefold ministry people; He is God for everyone.

If you don't know the following two things you won't know what is likely to come your way in the form of tests and trials, for that, you might be easily blindsided by devil tactics.

1. Who you are to God, and who you are in the plan of God.
2. What idols, demons, devils are already **IN** you to oppose who you are and who you are to become for the sake of the plan of God.

Because we are born into sin and shaped in iniquity, that stuff is preprogrammed into us, and the devil wants to put up a block to oppose you and the plan of God before you know who you even are.

You are saved – Hallelujah, amen --- When you know God and know who you are in Him, you can be prayed up and ready if, more like *when* adversity comes the adversary will have nothing in you, in the Name of Jesus. Amen.

We can't be so lazy or foolish as to have God just sitting there, taking Him for granted. If that happened to you, and you were invited, you'd be angry and leave. Look how stupid we'd be for not tapping into the power that is available for us to fight spiritual battles. Not only that, idol *gods* are probably laughing at mankind who is embracing *idols* as **God**, and reducing the Only Living God down to an idol. Talk about an evil exchange.

How do you think you would feel if someone invited you to their house and ignored you, took you for granted, and just had you sitting there? God does not waste--, not time, energy, power, or anointing, so don't you do it either.

Help!

God said He would never leave or forsake us. You're at your friends' house, for example, and you can help them. Instead, they just have you sitting there watching them go through issues, situations and problems. You can really help them, but they are not asking you anything. They are just complaining, suffering, and going *through* while lesser *gods* steal from you waiting for the opportunity to kill and destroy.

This is what God is doing in a stagnant situation, in the life of a person who is saved, but they are not appropriating Christ, and not calling on the Lord in their time of need. They haven't practiced the presence of God or the disciplines of prayer, faith or worship, so it is not a reflex or a natural thing for them to call on the Lord. They just have God sitting there as if He is an idol, but He is not an idol. He is the Only Living God

So, one fine day you got saved. Hallelujah, Praise the Lord, AMEN. That should **solve** everything, *right*? That could be why the "saved" person is not *practicing* Christianity, they think all is automatically done for them once they got saved. This could be why they are going *through* because they don't know God and are not calling on the Lord, even though they are saved, or profess to be so.

Erroneously, many think getting saved simply solves everything. Well, it *can* solve everything. Because being saved gives the power, the ability, the grace, the authority to solve everything. The first **_everything_** you must solve is the problems in your house – yes, your house. I mean the house that is <u>you</u>, your body, the house that houses your spirit and your soul.

Your spirit is regenerated when you get saved – thank You, Jesus. The other two aspects of yourself need to be dealt with: your flesh and your soul. **Idols ae demons, idols are devils, idols are little g *gods* and they must be cleared out of your soul.**

Bring your flesh under. Mortify it. KILL IT (not literally) but kill the lusts of your flesh. Let the body know that it's not running this anymore–, like it used to, when you were out in the streets, running with your unsaved *friends*.

Therefore, dear brothers and sisters, you have no obligation to do what your sinful nature urges you to do. For if you live by its dictates, you will die. But if through the power of the Spirit you put to death the deeds of your sinful nature, you will live. For all who are led by the Spirit of God are children of God.
(Romans 8:12-14)

You need to prosper your soul. **You** do it. You possess ye your soul. You possess your soul in sanctification and honor. Your will is part of your soul, so if you desire that the idols stay, they will. If you desire that they go, they must go, by resistance, deliverance, prayer, and fasting, or some combination of those things.

Beloved I pray above all things that you would prosper and be in health, even as your soul prospers. (3 John2)

Be in health and prosper as it relates to your soul means that the idols, idol *gods*, demons, devils have to GO. **You** must make them go, or at least acknowledge that they are there, stop serving them, resist the devil and he will flee. Seek and accept deliverance to **make** them go. By deliverance kick them out, then you must resist sin to keep them out.

Demons and devils cause disease. Most diseases have a spiritual cause. This is why Jesus cast out devils in His ministry—, He healed all that were oppressed of the devil.

> How God anointed Jesus of Nazareth with the Holy Ghost and with power: who went about doing good, and healing all that were oppressed of the devil; for God was with him.
> (Acts 10:38)

Just As We Are

God is not going to hand prosperity over to devils, demons, and idols --- that's why they come to rip you off, because God is not going to hand them blessings. So, these devils come, and they lodge in your soul to steal, kill, and destroy. They steal money, success, happiness, virtue, stars, marriages, education, family, money; they will steal anything that can be stolen. They also want not only your worship, they also want all the blessings that God has for you.

The only way they can get blessings that come from God is to steal them from the man whom God has blessed.

You must get rid of those devils.

Beloved, be in health and prosper, even as your soul prospers –, so your soul needs to be cleaned up. That is what you do after salvation instead of running around in the streets with your unsaved friends collecting more devils.

If we think about this, have we really invited Jesus into *our* hearts? *Our* hearts filled with all the things a heart is filled with?

> The heart is deceitful above all things, and desperately wicked: who can know it? I the LORD search the heart, I try the reins, even to give every man according to his ways, and according to the fruit of his doings.
> (Jeremiah 17:9-10)

Would you have a friend over without cleaning your house first?

Don't answer that – because some people would.

Come as you are and just as you are – well we have to because we have no power to rid ourselves of devils, demons and idol *gods* before salvation. We expose our souls really and invite Jesus into our hearts and life just as we are that fine day or night that we get saved.

In Salvation that is how it has to be. Reverend Billy Graham, who is credited for leading millions and millions to salvation always had a certain hymn sung when making the altar call.

This song was written by Charlotte Elliott when she felt alone and isolated. She recalled that when she received salvation she was told to come just as she was.

Saints of God that is our only option when the Holy Spirit convicts us of sin and that we are sinners. If we could clean up the mess we've made of things by the time we accept salvation, we wouldn't have made that mess. But only Jesus can regenerate our wicked spirits when we become born again, and become a new creature in Christ.

🎵 JUST AS I AM

Just as I am, without one plea
But that Thy blood was shed for me
And that Thou bid'st me come to Thee
Oh, Lamb of God, I come, I come

Just as I am, though tossed about
With many a conflict, many a doubt
Fighting and fears within without
Oh, Lamb of God, I come, I come 🎵

At salvation, if we have the faith for it, every demon, devil and idol *god* all can fall away, but we may be using all the faith we have just to be saved at that time. We may not know that there are demons, devils, or idols in our souls, we think that is just the way we are.

Even right after salvation, without knowing how to appropriate Christ, and having little word in us, we have little power, authority or ability (or inclination really) to get rid of these little g *gods*/idols and clean up our own soul.

So, we have no choice other than to come just was we are to that altar. Becoming a new creature in Christ is a prophetic statement, it is a process, and it takes time and effort on our part.

Lord, help us! Lord, Thank You!

We receive salvation and then immediately the Light of the Lord Jesus Christ informs us that we need to clean up our houses, now that we are in Christ and Christ is in us. And we realize that we have a way to do that. If we never do that, do we think that Christ would want to exist in the squalor day after day, week after week, year after year, in the heart of some of our souls?

If we don't stop the idolatry, then the *idols* get stronger in us, and they get further embedded in our souls.

Let's put it this way – if you were married to the love of your life but they still had an old flame that they kept around, talked about, went to see about from time to time, how do you think your marriage would be?

If you were married to the Love of your life and you two live together as a husband and wife should, but your spouse is out in the streets chasing whatever idolatrous people chase, how long do you think your marriage would last?

In Hosea 4:15 it reads that Israel plays the harlot. He says harlots but He's talking about idolatry. God hates harlotry. God hates idolatry. There are idols in our souls, things we like to do, like to look at, like to eat. There are people we like to--, love to--, are intensely passionate to defend, worship, look at, drool over, lust after, listen to, *support*. Those are idols.

Sex is a huge idol. Idols are not just tangible things you can hold in your hands.

So, people we know and also people that we may only know of, such as celebrities and public figures can also be idols.

God hates idolatry.

Sometimes that's why certain people in our life are no longer in your life; GOD HATES IDOLATRY. People can be idols, and God can also remove them. Money is huge idol to lots of people, and God will remove that too, if you don't put money in it's place in your life, but instead idolize it.

Let the Light of the Lord Jesus Christ shine deeply in your heart and check to see if you are guilty of the First

Commandment, and also the number one thing that God hates, because that could be the number one cause of all that stuff that happens to you in your life.

Clean Up Prayers

We are going to do some foundational prayers that I am calling Clean Up Prayers because they sweep the house we live in. When we are dealing with buildings and houses, we don't decorate before we make sure the foundation is right, and the house is clean.

1. Lord, let my enemies be silenced forever, in the Name of Jesus.
2. Lord, I repent for my sins, the sins of my parents and the sins of my ancestors, in the Name of Jesus.
3. Lord, remove all iniquity from my bloodline, in the Name of Jesus.

4. Lord, I repent all the way back to Adam and Eve where I retrieve my glory and my essence, in the Name of Jesus.
5. Thank You, Lord.
6. Holy Ghost Fire fall on these prayers, in the Name of Jesus.
7. Lord, let my enemies be silenced forever, in the Name of Jesus.
8. Lord, let your Hand be lifted up against my adversaries and let my enemies be cut off, in the Name of Jesus.
9. Thank You, Lord for Your protection, in the Name of Jesus.
10. Thank You Lord, for Your Love for me, in the Name of Jesus.
11. Thank You, Lord that You will never leave or forsake me, or leave me in the hands of the enemies of my soul, in the Name of Jesus.
12. Lord Jesus, have Mercy upon me; save me from the hands of my enemies, in the Name of Jesus.

13. Lord Jesus, forgive me for every sin, in the Name of Jesus.
14. Lord, let your hands of Mercy bring victory to me in every area of my life, in the Name of Jesus.
15. I drink the Blood of Jesus that my soul takes on the nature of Christ, in the Name of Jesus.
16. Blood of Jesus build a wall of defense around me, in the Name of Jesus.
17. Holy Ghost Fire, Holy Ghost Fire, Holy Ghost Fire, burn to ashes every weapon fashioned against me, in the Name of Jesus.
18. Lord, by the Fire of the Holy Ghost, make me hot for the things of the Kingdom, and never lukewarm, in the Name of Jesus.
19. Holy Spirit, protect me in my daily activities, in the Name of Jesus.
20. Holy Spirit empower me and fight with me to silence my enemies, in the Name of Jesus.

21. Lord, protect me from the snares of the fowler and the noisome pestilence, in the Name of Jesus.
22. Lord, fight for me, fight for me against my enemies, in the Name of Jesus.
23. Lord, silence my enemies forever, never let me have to look in their face again, in the Name of Jesus.
24. Lord, reveal the secret problems in my foundation that are hurting my life. Lord give me the words so that the enemy cannot resist so I can be saved, fully delivered, and converted, in the Name of Jesus.
25. Lord, let Your Holy Ghost Fire burn down all the enemy camps around me, in the Name of Jesus.
26. Lord, weaken, kill, and dry up the source of the enemy's power against me, in the Name of Jesus.
27. Lord, let the power of the wicked reverse and consume the wicked, in the Name of Jesus.

28. Lord, let the power of the wicked against me, reverse and consume the wicked, in the Name of Jesus.
29. Lord, do not allow my enemies to know peace until they surrender, in the Name of Jesus. (X2)
30. Evil serpents and scorpions that swallow my glory, vomit them up again, by Fire, by Force, in the Name of Jesus.
31. Any power sitting on an evil mat to interfere in my life, die on your mat, in the Name of Jesus.
32. Powers assigned to ruin my destiny, reverse your steps, and die, in the Name of Jesus.
33. Wicked instructions released to torment my life, backfire, in the Name of Jesus.
34. Demonic powers supporting household enemies against me, die, in the Name of Jesus.
35. Spirit hunters hunting for my soul, my life is not your candidate, die, in the Name of Jesus.

36. Unrepentant enemy around me clear away by the East Wind of God, in the Name of Jesus.
37. Witchcraft judgment against me in the spirit be nullified, in the Name of Jesus.
38. Angel of God invade the camp of my enemy and scatter them, in the Name of Jesus.(x2)
39. Powers assigned to turn the clock of my life backward, die, in the Name of Jesus.
40. Powers assigned to naked me, die, in the Name of Jesus. (X2)
41. Witchcraft ammunition and weapons set aside to fight me, catch Fire, catch Fire, catch Fire, and burn to ashes, in the Name of Jesus.
42. Hammer of God break to pieces every stone of hindrance on my way, in the Name of Jesus.
43. Thunder of God, arise and waste my enemies, in the Name of Jesus.

44. Witchcraft powers fighting my destiny, die, in the Name of Jesus.
45. Problem expanders in my life, die, in the Name of Jesus.
46. Arrows of shame fired against me to lose helpers and sink my destiny, backfire, in the Name of Jesus.
47. Every voice from the pit of hell shut up, shut up, in the Name of Jesus.
48. Enemies that surround me to harm me, die, in the Name of Jesus.
49. Old foundation in my life keeping me hostage, be replaced by the miracle foundation of God, in the Name of Jesus.
50. Every ancient gate holding me backward, I pull you down; scatter, in the Name of Jesus.
51. Every power standing in my way to obtain favor, die, in the Name of Jesus.

52. Every power holding evil vigil to scatter my destiny, die, in the Name of Jesus.
53. Every chain of darkness used to tie me down, break, break, break, in the Name of Jesus.
54. Every river of darkness flowing into my life, dry up, in the Name of Jesus.
55. Every attack of the enemy coming at me to block opportunities, scatter, in the Name of Jesus.
56. Every battle at the edge of breakthrough waiting to consume my joy, scatter, in the Name of Jesus.
57. Every strongman and strongwoman supervising my destiny, die, in the Name of Jesus.
58. Every sickness of darkness allotted to me by Satan and his agents, my life is not for you--, you die, in the Name of Jesus. (X2)

59. Every enchantment fired against my breakthrough, backfire, in the Name of Jesus.
60. All strange money that I have received that is now troubling my finances and wealth, your time is up, let that *spirit* go back and kill your owner, in the Name of Jesus.
61. Every satanic arrow fired against me, backfire, in the Name of Jesus.
62. Every siege of darkness waiting for my destruction, collapse, in the Name of Jesus.
63. Every power harassing my life, your days are numbered, die, in the Name of Jesus.
64. Every destructive incantation spoken to derail my life, backfire, in the Name of Jesus.
65. Every *spirit of Goliath* after my David, die--, I cut off your head, in the Name of Jesus.
66. Every *spirit of Herod* after the Jesus in me, die, and be eaten up by worms, in the Name of Jesus.

67. Every *spirit of pharaoh* after my Israel, leave me alone, and die, in the Name of Jesus. (X2)
68. Every wicked power of my father's house troubling my soul and progress, die, in the Name of Jesus.
69. Every agenda of darkness assumed to cause stagnancy in my life, scatter, in the Name of Jesus.
70. Every dark power supervising and monitoring my work, business, or career, die, in the Name of Jesus.
71. Every serpent programmed to cause problems in my life, die, in the Name of Jesus.
72. Every curse programmed into my life to cause problems in my life, die, in the Name of Jesus.
73. Every fetish power around my star, die, in the Name of Jesus.
74. Every evil arrow fired to torment me, backfire, in the Name of Jesus.
75. Every evil arrow fired to afflict me, backfire, in the Name of Jesus.

76. Every evil arrow of death fired at me, backfire 1000 times, in the Name of Jesus.
77. Every plan of the enemy to reduce me to nothing, scatter, in the Name of Jesus.
78. Every satanic siren sent into my life to cause hypertension, your time is up, back to sender, in the Name of Jesus.
79. Every curse of failure assigned to me in the spirit, my life is not for you, catch Fire and roast to ashes, in the Name of Jesus.
80. Every *vampire spirit*, I kill you today, die, in the Name of Jesus.
81. Every agent of affliction assigned to torment me, die, in the Name of Jesus.
82. Satanic meeting dedicated to silence me and my family, scatter, in the Name of Jesus.
83. Every miracle-diverting *spirit* of my father's house, die, in the Name of Jesus.

84. Every evil gate blocking my moving forward in life, I bind your strong man and in Christ, I command you to lift up, and be ye lift up, in the Name of Jesus.
85. Every evil power boasting against my existence be put to shame, in the Name of Jesus.
86. Every wicked assignment assigned to scatter my destiny, backfire, in the Name of Jesus.
87. Every charm used against me, backfire against the owner of the charm, in the Name of Jesus.
88. Wicked powers assigned to eliminate my destiny, die, in the Name of Jesus.
89. Lord, empower me to stand against all the schemes and the rebellion of the enemy against my destiny, in the Name of Jesus.
90. Lord, I renounce, denounce, and divorce the idols of my father's house, in the Name of Jesus.

91. Lord, empower me to abandon the idols of my father's house, forever, in the Name of Jesus. (X3)
92. Powers that press me down in my sleep to steal from me, die, in the Name of Jesus.
93. Cobwebs of poverty that the enemy is using to torment me, catch Fire and roast to ashes, in the Name of Jesus.
94. Fountain of bitterness planted by the enemy in my life, dry up, in the Name of Jesus.
95. Power that wants me to wake up every morning and cry, you are not my God, you die, in the Name of Jesus.
96. Witchcraft dream manipulators assigned to manipulate my dreams, your time is up, die, in the Name of Jesus.
97. Anti-progress powers of my father's house that want me to be poor, die, in the Name of Jesus.

98. *Anti-repentant spirit* trying to drag me to the pit of hell, die, in the Name of Jesus.
99. Stronghold of darkness holding me captive, be pulled down, in the Name of Jesus.
100. God arise, God arise, and silence all hired spiritual consultants employed to torment and scatter my destiny, in the Name of Jesus.
101. Satanic visitors that visited my life in order to destroy it, die, in the Name of Jesus.
102. Coffin of darkness assigned to me in the spirit, catch Fire, catch Fire and roast to ashes, in the Name of Jesus.
103. I discredit and nullify all mock funerals against me, and send them back to their owner, in the Name of Jesus.
104. Lord, silence any voice of lamentation against me and send it

back to sender, in the Name of Jesus.

105. Powers that want me to struggle and struggle with no results, you, evil power quit my life right now and die, in the Name of Jesus.

106. Powers assigned to steal my glory and crush my hope, die, in the Name of Jesus.

107. Witchcraft padlock designed to padlock my destiny to make me experience failure in life, break, in the Name of Jesus.

108. Any power assigned to cause me pain and seize my laughter, enough is enough, in the Name of Jesus.

109. Dark powers assigned to incriminate my identity, die, in the Name of Jesus.

110. Ancestral witchcraft embargo placed on my bloodline attacking my destiny, break in the Name of Jesus. (X2)

111. Whatever will bring pain that the enemy wants to use to laugh me to scorn, expire, in the Name of Jesus.
112. Quencher of glory and star killers of my father's house, my life is not your candidate, leave me alone and die, in the Name of Jesus.
113. Terrifying Noise of the Lord, scare my enemies to desolation, in the Name of Yeshua (X2).
114. Vultures of darkness after my life in the spirit, my life is not for you, die, in the Name of Jesus.
115. Stubborn pursuers after my life, I dash your power to pieces, in the Name of Jesus.
116. Anointing of disgrace assigned to me to move from house to house, die, in the Name of Jesus.

117. Anointing of disgrace to make me beg for food, dry up and backfire, in the Name of Jesus.
118. Powers assigned to add problems to my life, die, in the Name of Jesus.
119. Power of darkness, you will not drag my soul to the grave, in the Name of Jesus (X3)
120. Lord, commit to me the secret of prosperity, in the Name of Jesus.
121. Lord, make me more than a conqueror, in You, in the Name of Jesus.
122. God of Elisha, arise and pursue my pursuer, in the Name of Jesus.
123. Safety, peace, and wealth make my life your home, in the Name of Jesus.(X2)
124. Lord, pour Your oil of victory, greatness and breakthrough upon my head, in the Name of Jesus.(X5)

125. My Father, send help to me in every area where I am lacking, in the Name of Jesus.
126. I am in Christ. I am in Christ. I am in Christ, I am all in. I renounce and reject every idol from my father's house, in the Name of Jesus.
127. I reject every demon, every devil, every idol, every evil *spirit*, in my soul. Get out! Get out, get out! I am in Christ. I am in Christ. I am all in, in the Name of Jesus.
128. Lord, pour Your oil of anointing on me and arise and fill me with laughter, fill my life with joy that supersedes all joy that I've ever known, in the Name of Jesus.
129. Lord, arise and fill my heart and my life with joy that it supersedes all previous joy that I have ever known, in the Name of Jesus.
130. Lord, stop me from going through all of this *stuff;* Lord, heal

my foundation, in the Name of Jesus.

131. Stop this stuff from coming to me; Lord change, transfuse my blood with the Blood of Jesus.

132. Lord, stop me from drawing temptations and sin *stuff* to me; transfuse my blood fully with the Blood of Christ, so my blood no longer attracts evil into my life, into my family's life, into my destiny, in the Name of Jesus.

133. God arise, let tears and shame and rejection expire permanently in my life, in the Name of Jesus.

134. Let me live and see the goodness of the Lord in the land of the living, and that I may declare His goodness and give my testimony, in the Name of Jesus.

135. God arise, God arise and prepare a table before me in the presence of my enemies, in the Name of Jesus. (X2)

136. Thank You, Lord.
137. I cancel all witchcraft prophecies pronounced against me, in the Name of Jesus.
138. My destiny, be filled with miracles that surpass explanation, in the Name of Jesus.
139. I declare to people and to Heaven that this siege is over in my life. These foolish things that happen to me--, it's over, in the Name of Jesus.
140. My destiny, be filled with breakthrough and success and victory and prosperity, in the Name of Jesus.
141. Thank You Lord, for answered prayer.
142. Thank You, Lord that by the power of the Only Living God, I shall experience the miracles of explosive prosperity and supernatural promotion, all to the Praise of Your Glory, in the Name of Jesus.

143. Lord, I seal these declarations across every realm, age, dimension and timeline--, past, present, and future, to infinity, in the Name of Jesus.
144. I seal them with the Holy Spirit of Promise and with the Blood of Jesus.
145. Any backlash because of this word, these prayers, decrees, declarations and deliverance, experience the Lord's vengeance for messing with a child of God.
146. May the Lord cause any retaliation to backfire against the sender--, to infinity, in the Name of Jesus, that they would know that Jesus Is Lord.

Some prayer points adapted from **Dangerous Prayers for the Firstborn,** by Tella Olayeri.

Dear Reader

Thank you for acquiring, reading, and sharing this book. I pray the Lord will bless you and keep you As He receives you in the Beloved, fully put on Christ and put off the old man, that is the old nature so you can be victorious over circumstances and happenstances in your life.

In the Name of Jesus,

Amen.

Dr. Marlene Miles

Other books by this author

AK: *The Adventures of the Agape Kid*

AMONG SOME THIEVES

Ancestral Powers https://a.co/d/9prTyFf

Backstabbers https://a.co/d/gi8iBxf

Barrenness, *Prayers Against* https://a.co/d/feUltIs

Battlefield of Marriage, *The*

Blindsided: *Has the Old Man Bewitched You?* https://a.co/d/5O2fLLR

Break Free from Collective Captivity

Caged Life https://a.co/d/0eKxbU9H

Casting Down Imaginations
https://a.co/d/1UxlLqa

Church Craft: Witchcraft In the Church

Churchzilla, The Wanna-Be, Supposed-to-be Bride of Christ

Curses of Blind Men

Demonic Cobwebs (prayerbook)

Demonic Time Bombs

Demons Hate Questions

Devil Loves Trauma, *The*

Devil Weapons: Unforgiveness, Bitterness,...

The Devourers: *Thieves of Darkness 2*

Do Not Swear by the Moon

Don't Refuse Me, Lord (4 book series)
https://a.co/d/idP34LG

Dream Defilement

The Emptiers: *Thieves of Darkness, 1*
https://a.co/d/5I4n5mc

Every Evil Arrow
https://a.co/d/afgRkiA

Evil Touch https://a.co/d/gSGGpS1

Failed Assignment
https://a.co/d/3CXtjZY

Fantasy Spirit Spouse
https://a.co/d/hW7oYbX

FAT Demons (The): *Breaking Demonic Curses*

The Fold (5-book series)

- The Fold (Book 1)
- Name Your Seed (Book 2)
- The Poor Attitudes of Money (3)
- Do Not Orphan Your Seed (4)
- For the Sake of the Gospel (5)
- My Sowing Journal

Gang Ups: *Touch Not God's Anointed*

got HEALING? Verses for Life

got LOVE? Verses for Life

got HOPE? Verses for Life

got money? https://a.co/d/g2av41N

How to Dental Assist

How to Dental Assist2: Be Productive, Not Wasteful

Idols Are Demons, Idols are Devils, Idols Are Little-g *gods*

I Take It Back

In Multiplying, I Will Multiply Thee

Legacy (book 3 of the Upgrade Series)

Let Me Have A Dollar's Worth
https://a.co/d/h8F8XgE

Level the Playing Field
https://www.youtube.com/watch?v=BfF-TX1EWNQ

Living for the NOW of God

Lose My Location
https://a.co/d/crD6mV9

Man Safari, *The*

Marriage Ed. Rules of Engagement & Marriage

Made Perfect in Love

Money Hunters: Beware of Those

Money on the Altar https://a.co/d/4EqJ2Nr

Mulberry Tree https://a.co/d/9nR9rRb

Motherboard (The) - *Soul Prosperity Series*

Name Your Seed

Occupy: *Until I Return*

Plantation Souls

Players Gonna Play

Power Money: Nine Times the Tithe
https://a.co/d/gRt41gy

The Power of Wealth *(forthcoming)*

Powers Above

Repent of Visiting Evil Altars
https://a.co/d/3n3Zjwx

The Robe, *Part 1, The Lessons of Joseph*

The Robe, *The Lessons of Joseph* Part II,

Seasons of Grief

Seasons of Waiting

Seasons of War

Second Marriage, Third--, *Any Marriage*
https://a.co/d/6m6GN4N

Sift You Like Wheat

Six Men Short: What Has Happened to all the Men?

Son https://a.co/d/03NdPT2S

Soul Prosperity, Soul Prosperity Series Bk 3
https://a.co/d/5p8YvCN

Souls Captivity, Soul Prosperity Series Book 2

The Spirit of Poverty

StarStruck

SUNBLOCK

The Swallowers: *Thieves of Darkness*, Book 3

Take It Back

This Is NOT That: How to Keep Demons from Coming at You

Time Is of the Essence

Too Many Wives: *Why You Have Lady Problems*

Tormenting Spirits https://a.co/d/dAogEJf

Toxic Souls

Triangular Power *(series)*

- Powers Above
- SUNBLOCK
- Do Not Swear by the Moon
- STARSTRUCK

Uncontested Doom

Unguarded Hours, *The*

Unseen Life, *The* https://a.co/d/0drZ5Ll

Upgrade: How to Get Out of Survival Mode

- Toxic Souls (Book 2 of series)
- Legacy (Book 3 of series)

The Wasters: *Thieves of Darkness,* Bk 2
https://a.co/d/bUvI9Jo

What Have You to Declare? What Do You Have With You from Where You've Been?

When I Was A Child, *I Prayed As a Child*

When the Devourer is Rebuked

https://a.co/d/1HVv8oq

The Wilderness Romance *(series)*
This series is about conducting a Godly relationship and marriage with someone who is a Wilderness person. It is about how to recognize it and navigate through it. These books are about how not to get caught up in such.

- *The Social Wilderness*
- *The Sexual Wilderness*

- *The Spiritual Wilderness*

Other Series

The Fold (a series on Godly finances)
https://a.co/d/4hz3unj

Soul Prosperity Series https://a.co/d/bz2M42q

Spirit Spouse books

https://a.co/d/9VehDSo

https://a.co/d/97sKOwm

Thieves of Darkness series

Triangular Powers https://a.co/d/aUCjAWC

Upgrade (series) *How to Get Out of Survival Mode* https://a.co/d/aTERhX0

Prayer books by this author

While most books by this author have prayer points either throughout the book or at the end, there are some books that are **only** prayers. You just open up the book and pray. They are listed below:

Prayers Against Barrenness: *For Success in Business and Life*

Fruit of the Womb: *Prayers Against Barrenness*

Beauty Curses, *Warfare Prayers Against*
https://a.co/d/5Xlc2OM

Courts of Marriage: Prayers for Marriage in the Courts of Heaven
(prayerbook) https://a.co/d/cNAdgAq

Courtroom Warfare @ Midnight
(prayerbook) https://a.co/d/5fc7Qdp

Demonic Cobwebs *(prayerbook)*
https://a.co/d/fp9Oa2H

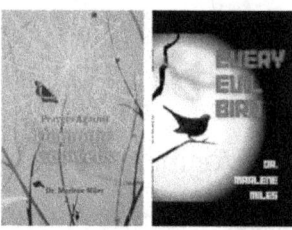

Every Evil Bird https://a.co/d/hF1kh1O

Every Evil Arrow
https://a.co/d/afgRkiA

Gates of Thanksgiving

Spirits of Death & the Grave, Pass Over Me and My House
https://a.co/d/dS4ewyr

*Please note that my name is spelled incorrectly on amazon, but not on the book.

Throne of Grace: Courtroom Prayer
https://a.co/d/fNMxcM9

Warfare Prayer Against Poverty
https://a.co/d/bZ611Yu

www.ingramcontent.com/pod-product-compliance
Lightning Source LLC
Chambersburg PA
CBHW061449040426
42450CB00007B/1283